BY THE AUTO EDITORS
OF CONSUMER GUIDE®

PORSCHE 911

BEEKMAN HOUSE
New York

Louis Weber, President
·Publications International, Ltd.
3841 West Oakton Street
Skokie, Illinois 60076

Permission is never granted for commercial purposes.

ISBN: 0-517-63668-9

Printed and bound by Zrinski, Yugoslavia
10 9 8 7 6 5 4 3 2 1

CONTENTS

Introduction **4**

Porsche Before The 911 .. **6**

The 911 GT Cars **11**

Carreras and Turbos **26**

The Ultimate 911: Type 959 .... **42**

911 Conversions **51**

911 Aftermarket **60**

Credits
Photography by Fred Heyler of Porsche + Audi of America; Martha A. McKinley of Porsche Cars North America, Inc.; and Klaus Parr of Dr. Ing. h. c. F. Porsche Aktiengesellschaft. Other photography by Vince Manocchi, p. 9; Dean Batchelor, p. 10; Roland Flessner, p. 24; Mel Winer, pp. 34-37; companies as listed under "911 Conversions"; Doug Mitchel, p. 53; Sam Griffith, pp. 54-59 (owner: Jean Banchet); David Gooley, pp. 55-56.

INTRODUCTION

Remember the first 911 that you ever saw or the first one that you ever drove? Maybe it was back in the mid-Sixties, when the styling was fresh and bold. Perhaps it was in the Seventies, when you wondered what kind of car would have such a strange-looking spoiler on the rear deck. It could have been in the Eighties, when wheel arch bulges, vents, and a slant nose caught your eye. Whether you've been an admirer since the first 911 stormed down a concrete slab or you've only just discovered the car, whether your interests are in the 911 as a racer or a street machine, you'll find more about it on the following pages.

The Porsche 911 and all of its variants were the inspiration of the man who gave the Volkswagen Beetle to the world—Dr. Ferdinand Porsche. He had consulted and worked for many manufacturers since the turn of the century. Porsche's two main interests were affordable transportation for the masses and racing sports cars. After World War II,

*Type 959 Porsche—the ultimate
development of the rear-engine,
rear-drive Type 911.*

the Volkswagen became a reality. Also, Ferdinand's
son Ferry and the reconstructed Porsche company
had begun plans for a sports car—as a project for
another company. When the sports car project didn't
go anywhere, Porsche developed the Type 356 itself,
and it eventually led to the Type 911.

Not only have the 911s proven themselves on race
tracks around the world, but the coupes and
cabriolets are known for their craftsmanship and
engineering. While the basic shape of the 911 hasn't
changed over the more than two decades in which it
has been built, with its hood slanting down between
the front fenders and its rounded and vented rear
deck, performance and handling improvements
abound.

The Type 911 is a dream car for most, something
that is a symbol of perfect sports car motoring.
Given its past history, there's every reason in the
world to think that it could go on forever—a fitting
tribute to the man whose name it carries.

PORSCHE
BEFORE THE 911

POSTWAR PORSCHE

After World War II, Porsche Konstruktionen GmbH, located in Gmünd, Austria, was managed by Ferry Porsche and his sister Louise Piech, along with Karl Rabe and Hans Kern. The latter two people were longtime friends and business associates of Ferry's father, Professor Ferdinand Porsche. The primary business of the company was engineering—design and consultation. Due to postwar restrictions, Ferry Porsche and Karl Rabe were unable to travel outside of Austria or Germany, and Ferdinand Porsche and Anton Piech were in prison because of "war crimes."

The company wanted representation in Italy, so Carlo Abarth and Rudolf Hruska were hired to seek customers for the Porsche design and engineering services. One of their first customers was Cisitalia, for which Porsche GmbH was to design a grand prix car, a small tractor, a sports car, and a water turbine. Part of the 1,000,000 French francs received as an advance for the work was paid to the French authorities to free Dr. Porsche and Anton Piech from prison, which took place on August 1, 1947.

On one of their first trips outside Germany, Ferry Porsche and Karl Rabe visited Cisitalia to check on the progress of the Type 360—the Cisitalia grand prix car. More interesting to Porsche and Rabe, though, was that Cisitalia had not gone ahead with

PROJECT NUMBER 356

the Porsche-designed sports car because it was having so much success with its own Fiat-based sports coupe.

The Cisitalia coupes and cabriolets were pretty cars, with Pinin Farina bodywork, and they were light, handled well, and were fairly fast. But they were also expensive to build, with their handmade tubular space frames. Piero Dusio, head of Cisitalia, had planned to build 500 of the cars, which were to sell for $5000 each in Italy and $7000 each in export markets. Porsche and Rabe were stunned to see a car with a Fiat 1100 engine, transmission, and rear axle selling for those prices, no matter how good-looking it was.

On their return to Gmünd, Porsche and Rabe dusted off some plans that had been lying dormant—plans for a Porsche-designed, Porsche-built sports car, having the project number 356. Their approach was more pragmatic than Dusio's had been for the Cisitalia because it involved the use of Volkswagen components. The VW parts not only fit their plan, but had been created by Ferry's father 10 years earlier.

The first Porsche was a roadster with an aluminum body designed by Erwin Komenda. The automobile utilized VW components—engine, transmission, brakes, wheels, and steering—but these were held together by a space frame, with the

MAJOR SPECIFICATIONS

1950 Porsche Type 356 1100 and 1965 Porsche Type 365C 1600SC		
General: Rear-engine, rear-drive, two-door sports cars. Unit bodies.		
Dimensions and Capacities	**1950 1100**	**1965 1600SC**
Wheelbase (in.):	82.7	82.7
Overall length (in.):	151.6	155.5
Overall width (in.):	65.4	65.7
Overall height (in.):	51.2	51.6
Track front (in.):	50.8	51.4
Track rear (in.):	49.2	50.1
Curb weight (lbs.):	1642	2061
Drivetrain		
Engine type: Horizontally opposed 4-cylinder, air cooled		
Displacement (cc/ci):	1086	1582
Compression ratio:	6.5:1	9.5:1
Fuel delivery:	2 Solex 32PBJ	2 Zenith 32NDIX
Net bhp @ rpm:	46 @ 4000 (SAE)	95 @ 5800 (DIN)
Transmission type:	VW non-synchromesh manual	Porsche all-synchromesh manual
Final drive ratio:	4.43:1	4.43:1
Chassis		
Front suspension:	Trailing arm, torsion bars	Trailing arm, torsion bars
Rear suspension:	Swing axle, torsion bars	Swing axle, torsion bars
Steering:	VW worm-gear	ZF
Brake system:	Ate hydraulic	4-wheel discs
Performance		
Top speed (mph):	90	116

engine in front of the rear axle. The car was taken to Switzerland in July 1948 for the Swiss Grand Prix at Bern, where it could be seen by members of the automotive press, some of whom tested it for reports in their magazines. A week later, on July 11, the new Porsche won its first race—a "round the houses" event in Innsbruck, Austria—driven by Professor Porsche's nephew, Herbert Kaes.

The space-frame design wasn't practical for mass production, so a new design was created—the 356/2, which had the engine placed behind the rear axle as it was in the Volkswagen. The "frame" for the first production Porsche was built up from sheet steel into a platform with welded box-section side sills and with a central tunnel adding stiffness and allowing room for wiring and controls to run from the front to the rear of the car. A coupe and cabriolet were planned. Austrian production of the 356/2 was only 4 cars in 1948, 25 cars in 1949, and 18 cars in 1950. By the spring of 1951, Porsche had sold only 51 cars—43 coupes and 8 cabriolets. Six cabriolets were bodied by Beutler and two by Porsche, as were all of the coupes. The problem centered in slow-moving body construction, which was all handmade.

*Opposite page, top: Ferry Porsche
in more recent times. Bottom:
Erwin Komenda, the designer of
the first aluminum-bodied
Porsche roadster. Below: One of
the last Type 356s built,
a 1965 Porsche 356C.*

DR. ING. H.C.F. PORSCHE KG, STUTTGART-ZUFFENHAUSEN

The Porsche family had wanted to move the company back to Stuttgart, where it had been prior to World War II, and it accomplished the two-stage move in 1949 and 1950. The first stage was to rent 5000 square feet of space in Reutter's plant to perform final assembly work. Then the company purchased an 1100-square-foot building that would become offices and design space. The company operated under the official name of Dr. Ing. h.c.F. Porsche KG in Stuttgart-Zuffenhausen.

The year 1950 was a significant one for Porsche. The first Stuttgart-built 356 rolled out of the plant on the day before Good Friday. Professor Porsche's 75th birthday was celebrated on September 3, and a month later, at the Paris Auto Salon, two Porsches were shown, marking the 50th anniversary of the first Porsche-designed car's debut at the Universal Exposition of Paris in 1900—the car was the electric

Lohner-Porsche. Unfortunately, Professor Porsche suffered a stroke in November 1950, and succumbed to his illness on January 30, 1951.

Production on the 356 series stopped in September 1965, after 15½ years and 76,303 Porsches of types 356, 356A, 356B, and 356C. Factory records indicate that 10 more Type Cs were built for special customers in 1966, but those records don't mention the names of the customers. During the first 15½ years, Porsche coupes and roadsters were driven successfully on the tracks, and they endeared themselves to those who bought them for the highway. The Type 356 Porsches established the marque in the minds of enthusiasts everywhere, paving the way for the extraordinary Porsche automobiles to follow.

THE 911
GT CARS

PORSCHE TYPE 695/901/911

The 911 had its origins in Type 695, the project that also produced Porsche's disc brakes. Its body, designed under Butzi Porsche's direction, was given the factory code designation T-7 (T-6 was the final development of the Type 356 that had appeared back in 1961). Butzi's assignment (from his father, who was not a body designer but knew what he wanted) was to give the car 2+2 seating, more cargo capacity, and a family resemblance to

the 356. Without greatly extending the familiar wheelbase, Butzi did a remarkable job in blowing out the interior to 2+2 proportions. The Type 695 had a low beltline, lots of glass, including a huge wrapped backlight, and a severely sloped front "hood." The front fenderline remained high and prominent, something Butzi considered a Porsche trademark. Because of its comparatively large greenhouse, the 695 prototype looked a little unorthodox, but it was distinctively Porsche. Its styling from the cowl forward survived in the production 911 almost intact. Eventually, the 695 was redesignated Type 901. With smoother rear styling and ovoid rear windows, both of which complemented the fastback roof treatment, the 901 was displayed at the Frankfurt Automobile Show in the autumn of 1963. Porsche told everyone at Frankfurt that the new car was being shown a year early. Production, it claimed, would not begin sooner than the summer of 1964.

Porsche is widely believed to have neatly arrived at its 901st project number in time to coincide with the appearance of the all-new road car. In fact, the numbering worked out a different way: Over the years, the factory has not been consistent or absolutely sequential in its numbering system, and quite a few numbers have been skipped. Ferdinand Porsche's first was Type 7—he didn't want anybody to think that he was just starting out. The number 901 was chosen to suggest a fresh start and a new direction, but that's all that there was to it. Ultimately, 901 became 911 because of protests from Peugeot, which had been using three-digit numbers with middle zeros on a number of cars, and it promised to prevent Porsche from selling the 901 in France unless the number were changed. (Zuffenhausen had a last word of sorts by giving a half-dozen competition models middle-zero numbers, as in the case of the beautiful 904 GTS.)

Lovable as it had been, the 356 would hardly be

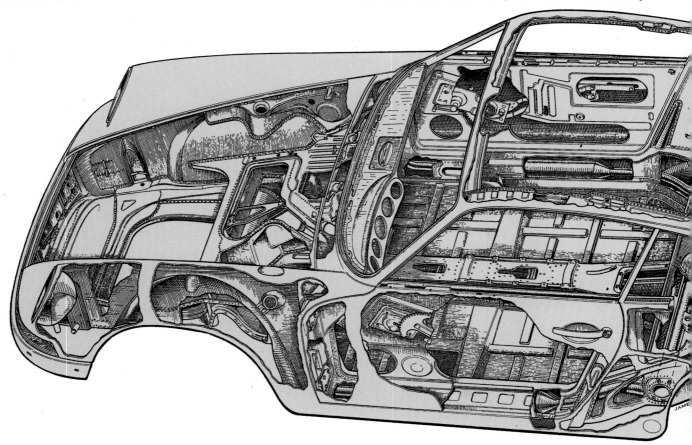

Bottom: The unit body of the 911.
Below: The 1964 Type 904 has a
1966cc flat four-cylinder engine that
develops 180-195 bhp at 7000 rpm.
Top speed is 160 mph.

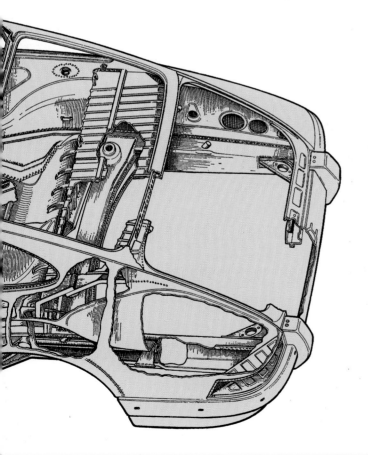

described as beautiful. But the 911 was. It remains a stunning design, arguably one of the most handsome sports/GT road cars in history. Mechanically, the 911 made a clean break from the 356 in several ways. The 911 was the first production Porsche to drop the swing-axle rear suspension and trailing-arm front suspension, though it retained the 356's torsion bars for springing. It was the first production Porsche with six cylinders, though the engine remained a horizontally opposed air-cooled unit mounted at the rear as per 356 practice, behind the rear axle centerline. Unlike the 356, however, it was supported at both ends—by the transaxle unit in front and a transverse mount in the back. Like previous Porsches, the 911 had an all-synchromesh transmission with an overdrive top gear, but now there were five ratios instead of four, providing greater flexibility than ever before.

The 901 wheelbase was 86.8 inches, up 4.1 inches from the 356C—hardly what could be called a four-passenger model. The suspension of the new Porsche was a complete departure for the company. At the front were MacPherson struts—something new at the time—and wishbones connected to longitudinal torsion bars. Rear suspension comprised transverse torsion bars and semi-trailing arms. Another change on the 911 was steering, now ZF rack-and-pinion instead of the old VW-based worm gear mechanism. Thus vanished one of the last remnants of the original Porsche/VW kinship. The steering was light, shock-free, and had plenty of surface feel. Much of its shock-free nature could be attributed to the hydraulic shock absorber in the linkage.

The heart of the 911 was, of course, its new single overhead cam 2.0-liter flat-six, with one camshaft per cylinder bank driven by a pair of double roller chains rather than the complicated multiple bevel gears of the four-cam flat-fours. The 911's six-throw crankshaft had no fewer than eight main bearings. A countershaft was mounted underneath to carry

impulses to twin chain sprockets at its rear end, each sprocket driving a camshaft. Ahead of the countershaft were two oil pumps, a large scavenger circulating oil from the dry sump to the tank and back, and a smaller unit maintaining lubrication pressure. An oil cooler was fitted, and Porsche instructed that oil temperature should never rise above 130° F. No tester ever recalled that it did.

On the 901/911, a rear seat was retained as on the 356, though the seatbacks were individually hinged for greater versatility in carrying cargo and passengers. Despite the production car's more streamlined rear compared to that of the Type 695

prototype, an adult or two children had room to sit in back. Porsche had taken pains to supply a really competent heating system for the interior. Now, air was taken from the cooling fan through a heat box and rammed into the cockpit via heater and defroster outlets. An option was a gasoline heater with an electric fan that forced more air into the heating boxes, though once the car was warmed up and moving, the fan was rarely necessary. Porsche had also improved interior airflow by adding extractor vents above the backlight. Another notable aspect of the interior was the dashboard, which seemed relatively bland compared with the

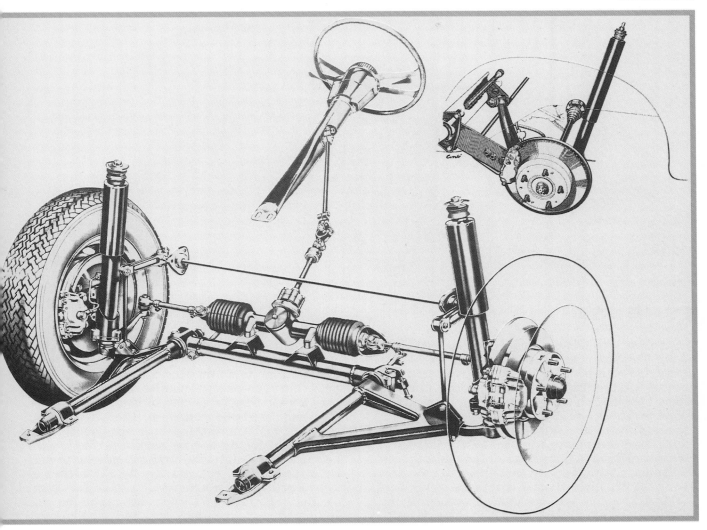

by-then almost classic 356 control board. On top was a molded full-width crash pad. Ahead of the steering wheel was an oblong binnacle housing five circular gauges. The largest was the tachometer, mounted dead center, flanked on the left by combination dials for oil/fuel levels and oil pressure/temperature, and on the right by the speedometer and an electric clock. Below the cluster was a panel with teakwood trim containing various minor knobs and switches. The expected shapely bucket seats had adjustable backrests.

As was the case with every evolution of the 356 before it, the 911 received a somewhat mixed reception

from confirmed Porsche fans, most of whom later grew to accept it—and inevitably to respect it. The 911 would prove to be the most popular Porsche in history, a title that it still holds despite the advent of the front-engine cars. Porsche's biggest problem with the 911 was adequate supply, because demand for it was strong from the outset. In mid-1963, the company bought Reutter, which assured better quality control, but did nothing to increase production capacity. In the end, Porsche contracted with Karmann to supply 911 bodies, a move that effectively forced the 356C to be phased out. Production of the 356 ended in September 1965.

TYPE 912

But a four-cylinder car would still be a part of the lineup. This new model was designated Type 912, although (as with the 911 on which it was based) the number was originally 10 digits below that in actual order. Porsche "officially" introduced both cars at the same time in late 1964, with one works representative stating that he was afraid new car announcements were becoming a habit at Zuffenhausen— "We only had one 15 years before." The sale of 911s in the United States began in early 1965, but the first 912s weren't delivered until June of the same year.

The 912 engine was a detuned version of the 1600SC unit from the last of the 356 series, developing 102 brake horsepower (DIN) at 5800 rpm. On paper, the 912's performance should not have been as exhilarating as the SC's because the new body shell was heavier and curb weight was about 100 pounds higher. But the 912 was offered with the 911's five-speed gearbox as a $75 option, and it had better aerodynamics than the 356C. Thus, the 912 actually had a higher top speed than the old Super 90. Its typical 0-60 mph acceleration time was 11.5 to 12 seconds, and it could run the quarter-mile from a standing start in a shade over 18 seconds at about 77 mph. Top speed was approximately 120 mph, though the factory's official quote was a conservative 116 mph. The 911 could hit 125 mph with its 150-bhp flat six. Predictably, the 912 was

much thriftier than the 911—25 mpg was the overall average.

Aside from its slower acceleration and lower top speed, the 912 was quite similar to the 911 in most other areas of performance: In both, brakes were strong and well-nigh fade-free. The new steering was light and transmitted little road shock. The German Dunlop SP radials worked perfectly with the suspension to provide strong cornering power. Some specification changes for the 912 helped to keep its price down to under $4700 POE: For example, the 911's teakwood lower dash appliqué was eliminated, as were the clock and oil temperature/pressure dial. The 912's tachometer was front and center as in the 911, but it was accompanied only by a speedometer and the combination temperature and fuel level gauge. Warning lights monitored everything else.

At the 1965 Frankfurt exhibition, Porsche showed a prototype for a second 901-series body style with built-in rollbar, which became the well-loved Targa cabriolet. Available in both 911 and 912 versions, it was introduced for export markets in 1967. Butzi Porsche had objected to retaining the coupe's rear sheet metal on this model, saying that a conventional "trunked" style was the only proper one for a cabriolet. But the company envisioned much lower sales for the Targa, which made shared

*The 912's coupe body style (opposite
page) was supplemented by the Targa
cabriolet (below) starting in 1967.
The roll bar is finished in brushed
stainless steel. Fixed glass rear
windows eventually replaced the
early zip-out plastic ones.*

rear bodywork mandatory. The good side to the economy measure was that it inspired Butzi to design into the car a strong, functional roll bar. Initially, the Targa had a zip-out plastic rear window and a removable folding roof panel made of rubberized fabric. The roll bar itself was finished in brushed stainless steel, chosen, said Butzi, to emphasize the functionality of the roll bar.

Once the final figures were in, the public seemed to have wanted Targas in far greater numbers than Porsche had anticipated, and the Targa's initial share of only 12.7 percent of production proved inadequate. Porsche also found that the 912 models sold much better than the 911s, not too surprising in view of the 911's price. Of nearly 13,000 cars built in 1966, over 9000 were the four-cylinder sort. But these were the problems of success, ones that everyone at Porsche was happy to endure. The 911 and 912 were solid hits. It hadn't been easy to follow a legend—but the company succeeded.

TYPE 911s

With the advent of three 911s for the 1968 model year, changes in Porsche model designations became increasingly difficult to follow—if not for the Porschephile, then surely for the layman. Actually, the year-to-year revisions weren't all that complicated and, being Porsche, were made in a perfectly logical fashion.

The first offshoot of the original 911 was the 911S, announced for the 1967 model year, with a base price of just over $7000. That made it the most expensive Porsche in history, though far more astronomical prices were coming. With the 911S, Porsche effectively reestablished the three-tier lineup of earlier years: The logical building blocks of 356 Normal, Super, and Super 90 were now the 912, 911, and 911S. To make room for the S, Porsche detrimmed the normal 911 to 912 standards (except for instrumentation, carpeting, and insulation) and cut base price by about $320, thus neatly splitting the difference between the $4700 912 and the $7074 911S.

The 911S was a hot car, thanks to changes in carburetion, compression ratio, and valve timing. The compression ratio was raised from 9.0 to 9.8:1, and the Weber carburetors, while essentially no different from those adopted for the normal 911 in early 1966, had larger jets. Although the S packed more horsepower (190 DIN compared to 130 on the 911), the big change was in torque, which peaked much higher (5200 rpm vs. 4300 rpm). As on other models, there was no choke, but pumping the accelerator was usually sufficient for starting—and also

helped cause chronic plug fouling, which proved a problem.

The 911S was a free-revving, tremendously potent car. The slightest blip of the throttle was enough to send the tach needle scurrying to its 7300-rpm redline. Recognizing this propensity, Porsche

installed an ignition cutout on the rotor arm, which effectively shut everything down if you approached the limit, protecting the valve gear from the overly enthusiastic. The only other mechanical change of importance for the S involved the brakes, which had ventilated rather than solid rotors for better fade resistance, having the complementary effect of raising pedal effort.

Came 1968 and the 911S, so recently introduced, vanished from the States as suddenly as it had appeared. Ostensibly, the reason was U.S. emission controls, but some sources say that the reason was the plug fouling, which had proven a tremendous service problem. The 911S would return to the United States a year later, although it continued in Europe. Meantime, the place of the 911S was left open.

TYPE 911L

The 911L replaced the standard 911 just after the model year began. The L (for *Luxus*, luxury) was essentially the same car as the S except that it used the normally tuned engine. It was an upmarket move for Porsche, because it sold the 911L for $600 more than the previous year's base 911. Some of the increased price had gone into modifications for meeting new federal safety and emissions regulations. More of the same would be seen in future years.

Of special interest for 1968 was a most unexpected development, designated Project Type 905 by the factory: It was an automatic transmission, called Sportomatic by Zuffenhausen. More precisely, it

was a semi-automatic, with a torque converter, automatic clutch, and manually shifted four-speed gear selector. The torque converter and clutch were supplied by Fichtel and Sachs, while the selector was Porsche's own creation. Gear ratios differed considerably from those of Porsche's fully manual four-speed, with the manual's final drive at 4.43 while the Sportomatic's was at 3.86. The Sportomatic-equipped 911L was commensurately slower in standing-start acceleration, but almost as fast at the upper end, with maximum converter efficiency being a very high 96.5 percent.

Learning to drive the new transmission, however, took a little practice, shifting without a clutch. In effect, Sportomatic was a compromise solution to the perennial problem of Americans lugging their cars in high gear at low speeds, fouling the plugs, and otherwise loading up the engines, all because drivers were loath to use the gearbox. The 4200-rpm torque peak meant lots of shifting on a manual car, but Sportomatic could take speeds as low as 20 miles per hour. Sportomatic was a typically well-conceived Porsche response to a perceived problem, and in practice it worked better than most automotive journalists expected. Fuel mileage wasn't hurt too much, and the transmission's effect

on performance was slight. Being able to disengage the clutch by the merest touch of the hand on the shift lever was disconcerting, but drivers became accustomed to it after brief experience. All in all, it was a novel idea, if not the kind of thing that would appeal to Porsche drivers.

TYPES 911T, 911E, 911S (RETURNED)

The confusion in Porsche's passenger car line soon ended. By 1969, a three-model 911 lineup returned. The 912, to be replaced in 1970 by the "Volks-Porsche" Type 914, was carried on unchanged. The trio of 911s continued for the next five model years. In ascending order of horsepower, they were the 911T, 911E, and 911S. Of these three, only the 911T was carbureted. Both the 911E and the reintroduced 911S utilized fuel injection, the intelligent answer to the emissions-control question. The injection system, developed by Porsche and Bosch, was a mechanical unit similar to that of Mercedes-Benz.

Horsepower was up on both the E and S, thanks to tuning changes made possible by the switch to injection. The 911E now had the same cam profile as the original 911, which was thus wilder than on the 911L. The S had no camshaft changes, but did get slightly higher compression and reshaped inlet passages, along with an extra oil cooler to guarantee reliability at the high power. Crankcases on all 911s were now made of magnesium rather than aluminum. This casting was supplied by Mahle of

Stuttgart. The carbureted 911T coupe sold for $5995, with the E and S coupes increasing to $7195 and $7895, respectively. Brake horsepower ran from 110 in the T to 140 in the E and 170 in the S.

The bodies of the 1969 models could be distinguished by slightly flared wheel openings and, though not immediately detectable, a longer wheelbase: The rear wheels had been moved back about 2.25 inches—a key change as far as improving weight distribution to 44/56 percent front and rear. Wheels and tires were wider, putting more rubber on the road and slightly increasing track.

By the 1973 model year, horsepower had increased in all three models, with the T at 140 bhp, the E at 165 bhp, and the S at 190 bhp. Changes in options had occurred, with the Boge self-adjusting hydropneumatic front suspension struts at first available for the cars, then dropped. A three-speed heater fan, flat-black wiper arms, and heated rear window were some of the refinements to be found in the 1969 model year, making it the most tractable and pleasurable touring Porsche since the 356C. The three 911s only continued to improve in their T, E, and S forms. Despite the increasing stranglehold of emissions requirements in the United States, the cars continued to be good performers.

By 1970—1972 at the latest—the whole 911 line had been carefully improved to a near-perfect state, just as the 356 had before it, by a small group of people in Stuttgart who were just a shade more serious about building automobiles than just about anybody else. One supposes that the T/E/S of these years were the reasons why there are still 911s today. After 1972, Porsche had only to keep doing everything it was doing already. It did—and still is.

TYPE 911 (AGAIN) AND 911S (CONTINUED)

Porsche juggled model designations and engine specifications confusingly once again for 1974. Starting at the bottom was a plain 911, equivalent to the previous T, followed by a 911S that was really much like the former E in performance and fuel economy. Both 911s shared the same engine, along with the newly introduced Carrera—one that produced up to 167 bhp (SAE) from 2.7 liters. The bore had been increased to achieve the larger displacement. The displacement boost was yet another response to tightening U.S. emissions standards, and was accompanied by a switch to Bosch CIS continuous fuel injection, replacing the previous mechanical system, plus minor tuning changes and a lower rev limit (down from 7000 to 6500 rpm).

Another sign of the times was evident outside, as all the 911s acquired redesigned safety bumpers. They were made of aluminum to save weight and were painted to match body color to save the car's

looks. Out back was a new full-width taillight lens bearing the Porsche name, along with black-finish engine lid louvers with chrome 2.7 logo. Inside were new high-back bucket seats, redesigned control knobs, tiny air vents at either end of the dash, and new steering wheels. Adoption of a smaller space-saver spare tire left room for a larger gas tank (by 4.7 gallons), and Targa models acquired a one-piece removable top.

The plain 911 disappeared in 1975, leaving the S

Opposite page, top: The first 911 Carrera was introduced in 1974, complete with aluminum safety bumpers. Middle and bottom: Recent cabriolet and Targa versions of the 911. Below, left: The dash of a 1986 911 has complete instrumentation. Controls remain similar to those found in the early 911s. New 911 Targa (below, right) and cabriolet (bottom, left) versions. Bottom, right: 3164cc engine develops 200 bhp.

the only alternative to the Carrera. From then through 1977, the 911S increased in price, though changed little mechanically or stylistically. In 1978, its successor—the 911SC—would start at over $22,000. But inflation was not confined to Porsche, and in many ways the 911SC remained something of a bargain. Throughout one of the most troubled periods for the automotive industry, when engineers and stylists had to bow to the wishes of politicians to sell their cars, Porsche managed to keep the 911 not

only within the requirements but just as exciting as it had always been. At the 25th anniversary celebration in May 1974, Ferry Porsche confirmed that the old warrior was far from finished: "With all the regulations that are known to us now, we think the 911 can keep going for the next six years." As usual, Ferry was being modest. In the autumn of 1983, the Porsche 911—on balance, one of the all-time automotive greats—had its 20th birthday. And it continues to thrill enthusiasts to this day.

Type 911 Carrera—today's base 911—looks much the same as the first 911s did in 1965. Wheelbase is 2½ inches longer and the six-cylinder engine has increased almost 1200cc.

TYPE 911 CARRERA TODAY

The current 911 offerings are the 911 Carrera coupe, targa, cabriolet, and the 911 Turbo. We'll address the Turbo in a chapter to follow. Ranging from about $35,000 and up, the 911s carry on the the body style begun in 1964. Their six-cylinder air-cooled engine displaces 3164cc and develops 200 bhp (SAE), burning unleaded regular gasoline. The 911s are still performers, clipping from 0-60 miles per hour in 6.3 seconds and reaching a top speed of 146 miles per hour, according to the factory.

Over the years, the 911 has earned countless admirers, justifiably continuing in its production because of demand by enthusiasts. While the car is enthralling in its road form, Porsche has accomplished wonders on it as a basis for even stronger performance, starting with the Carrera in 1973.

MAJOR SPECIFICATIONS

Selected 1965-86 Porsche Type 911 and Type 912

General: Rear-engine, rear-drive, two-door sports cars. Unit bodies.

Dimensions and Capacities	1965 911	1966 912	1966 911S	1969 911T/ 911E/911S	1978 911SC	1986 911
Wheelbase (in.):	87.0	87.0	87.0	89.3	89.5	89.5
Overall length (in.):	163.9	163.9	163.9	163.9	168.9	168.9
Overall width (in.):	63.4	63.4	63.4	63.4	65.0	65.0
Overall height (in.):	52.0	52.0	52.0	52.0	51.6	51.6
Track front (in.):	52.6	52.6	52.6	52.6	53.9	53.9
Track rear (in.):	51.8	51.8	52.2	51.8	54.3	54.3
Curb weight (lbs.):	2270	2100	2280	2280	2756	2756

Drivetrain

	1965 911	1966 912	1966 911S	1969 911T/ 911E/911S	1978 911SC	1986 911
Engine type(1):	6-cylinder	4-cylinder	6-cylinder	6-cylinder	6-cylinder	6-cylinder
Displacement (cc/ci):	1991/121.4	1582/96.5	1991/121.4	1991/121.4	2994/183.0	3164/193.2
Compression ratio:	9.0:1	9.3:1	9.8:1	8.6:1/9.1:1/ 9.8:1	9.3:1	9.5:1
Fuel delivery:	6 Solex 40PJ carbs	2 2-bbl Solex carbs	6 Solex 40PF carbs	Carbs/Bosch mech. fuel injection	CIS fuel injection	CIS fuel injection
Net bhp @ rpm:	130 @ 6100 (DIN)	102 @ 5800 (SAE)	160 @ 6600 (DIN)	110 @ 5800/ 140 @ 6600/ 170 @ 6800 (DIN)	172 @ 5500 (SAE)	200 (SAE)
Net lbs/ft torque @ rpm:	143 @ 4300 (SAE)	90 @ 3500 (SAE)	144 @ 5200 (SAE)	na	175 @ 4200 (SAE)	185 (SAE)
Transmission type:	5-speed manual, Sportomatic 4-speed semi-auto	4- or 5-speed manual	5-speed manual, Sportomatic 4-speed semi-auto	5-speed manual, Sportomatic 4-speed semi-auto	5-speed manual	5-speed manual
Final drive ratio:	4.43:1	4.43:1	4.43:1	4.43:1	3.8:1	3.8:1

Chassis

Front suspension: MacPherson strut, lower A-arms, coil springs, transverse torsion bars, anti-roll bar(2)
Rear suspension: Semi-trailing arm, transverse torsion bars(3)
Steering: Rack-and-pinion
Brake system: 4-wheel disc

	1965 911	1966 912	1966 911S	1969 911T/ 911E/911S	1978 911SC	1986 911
Wheels:	15"	15"	15"	14", 15" optional	15", 16" optional	15"
Tires:	6.95" × 15"	6.95" × 15"	6.95" × 15"	185/14, 185/70HR-14 optional E, 185/70HR-15 optional S	185/70VR-15 front, 215/60VR-15 rear; optional 205/55VR-16 front, 225/50VR-16 rear	185/70VR-15 front, 215/60VR-15 rear

(1) All engines have horizontally opposed cylinders and are air-cooled
(2) 1969 911T/E/S—Boge self-adjusting hydropneumatic struts optional
(3) 1966 911S, 1978 911SC, 1986 911—rear anti-roll bar

CARRERAS
AND TURBOS

THE CARRERA RS

The rationale that saw the name Carrera return to the Porsche lineup in 1973 was mainly competition, a subject Porsche had never ignored. The Carrera RSRs, which blew the wheels off of everything else in sight at races like that year's Daytona 24 Hours, were built to keep the Type 911 in the competition forefront. Dr. Ernst Fuhrmann, who became president of the company in 1972, decided that the second-generation road cars would remain in production well beyond the planned introduction of the front-engine Type 924.

The original Carrera RS concept was a stripped, lightweight 911-based model that could be homologated easily for Group 4 GT racing. The "customer" model had a special 2.7-liter engine (Type 911/93), developed by boring out the 2.4 six to 90mm—the main difference from the standard 911S engine. Both units had the same 8.5:1 compression ratio,

Bosch-Porsche fuel injection, valve sizes, and timing. The added displacement gave the RS power-plant 20 more horsepower.

Since it was destined for competition, the Carrera RS 2.7 was lightened drastically and, in some areas, ingeniously. For instance, Porsche used special thin steel and glass and fiberglass rear deck and rear aprons (the latter on racing models only). The cock-pit had no insulation, being very spartan: Rubber mats replaced carpets; the thin, detrimmed door panels had pull-cord door releases; there were thin bucket seats and no clock, passenger sunvisor, or nonfunctional trim.

The chassis was equipped with gas-pressurized Bilstein shock absorbers, extra stiff anti-sway bars, and aluminum rims—wider than the 911S at the rear, with fenders flared to accommodate them. The "ducktail" spoiler had been ordained by wind tunnel

experiments. It looked weird, but was brilliant in actual use, providing extra downforce to hold the tail firmly to the track at speed as well as increasing airflow through the engine cover's grillework.

Calling this car a Carrera was an obvious move that couldn't be faulted. The name had previously graced the most competitive of Porsches, not only the great four-cam 356s, but later the sports racing Carrera 904 GTs and the Type 906 Carrera 6. Stylists made the most of the name, with huge body-side graphics displaying the traditional Carrera script.

Porsche was required to build 500 RS Carreras for homologation purposes and, to make sure this quantity sold, the price was held down to about $10,000 in Germany. Production had to be increased

to 1000 and later 1800 to meet the demand. This brought with it an important side benefit: It allowed Porsche to homologate the car in Group 3 (series-production GT cars) where it required minimal race-preparation and stood to dominate the class rather than Group 4. With good sales, Porsche happily raised the price by several thousand dollars to more closely approximate the car's true worth.

The Carrera RS was greeted with high enthusiasm, which wasn't hard to muster once you got behind the wheel. Paul Frére in Belgium timed one from a standing start to 100 mph in 13 seconds flat, and registered a true top speed of 150 mph. Although his car was one of the ultralight RSR variations, the production job was hardly less impressive. None of the road testers could say that the RS

Opposite page: 1965 Porsche 904 at the Monte Carlo Rally. Below: 1966 Porsche 906. Bottom: 1974 Porsche 911 Carrera. Note blacked out trim, graphics, and bumpers different from European version on page 27.

Carrera was a cushy tourer, but all agreed that it was tractable for street use, where it delivered as much as 15 miles per gallon.

Thus established, the RS converted easily to Peter Gregg's Daytona-winning RSR—the all-out competition version. The RSR was entered at the Daytona 24-hour race by Brumos Porsche of Jacksonville, Florida. The RSR engine had 2806cc and a revised cylinder head with 10.5:1 compression. It produced an astounding 308 horsepower (DIN) at 6200 rpm,

and it would leap to 100 mph in about 12 seconds. It had a spendid Group 4 career, winning everything in sight in the IMSA Camel GT series and the Trans Am. In Europe, the RSR was GT Champion for 1973, vanquishing the favored de Tomaso Panteras. With some difficulty, the engine was enlarged to 2993cc by a further bore increase for the Martini Racing team. Now it developed 315 horsepower, and the car beat everything in sight at a four-hour race at Le Mans, blasting down the Mulsanne Straight at

The turbocharged Porsche Carrera (below) was the street version of the Carrera RSRs. The 2993cc engine (opposite page) could take the Carrera from 0-60 mph in anywhere from 4.9 to 6.7 seconds, depending on the driver.

up to 179 mph. Later Martini RSRs developed 330 bhp and, in more heavily modified form, entered Group 5, where they continued to excel.

For 1974, Porsche upped the ante all round with the Carrera RS 3.0, needing to build only 100 to homologate it as an "evolution" of the lightweight 1973 model. Incorporated were a wider, horizontal rear spoiler, wider wheels and tires, die-cast aluminum crankcase, and revised inner pivot points for the rear suspension. The 1973 model had required a spe-

cial permit in Germany owing to the huge spoiler, but the 3.0 had an alternate "street" spoiler, soon nicknamed the "whale tail," with a protective rubber safety surround. Lightening techniques gave the 3.0 a curb weight of only 2400 pounds. Available in a variety of wild colors, it was marked by black exterior trim—window moldings, rearview mirror, door handles, taillight housings. The engine developed 220/230 bhp on premium fuel, and Paul Frére averaged 124 mph on 78 miles of Italian

autostrada with one in mid-year. Roger Penske helped move out the 109 3.0s built by ordering 15 of them for his International Race of Champions. Another 50 were built with RSR specifications, the version that won the Trans Am and IMSA Camel GT series again, with Peter Gregg. In 1975, with the racing Type 934 Turbo still a year away, the Carrera RS/RSRs continued to dominate the European Hillclimb Championship, Daytona, and Le Mans, where one finished fifth overall.

Meanwhile, Porsche adopted the Carrera name for a new top-of-the-line road car that debuted in America for 1974. The U.S. Carrera shared its engine with the 911 and 911S of that model year— one of 2.7 liters that developed 167 bhp (SAE) for the S and the Carrera. The Carrera cost close to $14,000. The "tea tray" IROC-style engine lid spoiler was the main distinguishing point between the 1974 and

1975 Carreras. The '75 also had leather upholstery. From a performance standpoint, the 1974 Carrera was slightly better than the '75. The 0-60 mph time was up to 8.4 seconds against 7.4, and official top speed was down from 142 to 132 mph. Although Porsche continued to avoid the worst maladies of the emission control era, tighter 1975 regulations meant that the Carrera had 10 horsepower less than in 1974—15 less on California versions. But the dreaded catalyst had still been avoided: The 49-state cars didn't need it, and California models used twin thermal reactors and exhaust-gas recirculation. In tractability, however, the '75 was superior. It started easily from cold, behaved well in traffic, and offered plenty of low-end torque. For the Carrera's $1700 price premium over a 911S, the buyer received bodyside graphics with special colors, opening rear quarter windows, electric side

windows, RS-type black exterior trim, bulging fenders to accommodate the wider rear wheels, and a tray-like spoiler mounted at an upward angle on the engine lid. Chrome exterior trim could be ordered instead of black, if desired. On the inside, the Carrera could be distinguished by a three-spoke steering wheel, but was otherwise much like the 911S. Interiors were funereal at the time, as the government banned shiny materials, and matte-black rapidly replaced silver or chromium plate. Outside the United States, the Carrera had much more power and was a totally different car.

TYPE 930

Ernst Fuhrmann served as president of the Porsche company from 1972 to 1982. Fuhrmann had personally designed the four-cam engine for the 356 Carrera. He also directed design of the later 911-based RS and RSR Carreras. He knew and appreciated good engineers, and he hired many of them himself. He knew without doubt that racing really does improve the breed. And he also knew a good deal about turbochargers from Porsche's work on the tremendous 12-cylinder blown powerplant for the racing 917. Would a turbo-supercharger work on a Porsche 911? One of the first things that Fuhrmann did after becoming president was to set in motion a program to find out.

In 1973, Zuffenhausen displayed a "911 Turbo" at several European auto shows, but remained less than forthright about plans to produce it. In 1974, the Martini & Rossi team raced a turbocharged 2.1-liter 333-bhp Carrera RSR with mixed results. For instance, one was doing 189 mph on the Mulsanne

Straight at Le Mans when it threw a rod and retired. Based on experience with this racing turbo, Fuhrmann and company began readying a production version—a smooth, quiet, very fast coupe with a 234-bhp 3.0-liter 911 six. The Turbo Carrera debuted in Europe for the 1975 model year, and the American model was ready a year later. Enthusiasts owe a debt of thanks to Fuhrmann and his team, for they pressed on with the "street" Turbo in spite of the Arab Oil Embargo of 1973-74 and all that the embargo seemed to imply for the high-performance, high-thirst cars of that time. Fuhrmann's team did defeat the sales department's campaign to offer the

Turbo at an artificially low price. Fuhrmann felt that if Porsche were going to sell the car at all, then the company should go all out. It did.

The Type 930, as it was designated, packed in almost every luxury and convenience the factory could squeeze. Air conditioning, automatic heat control, AM/FM stereo (U.S. version), electric antenna and window lifts, leather upholstery, tinted glass all around, headlamp washers, rear window wiper, Bilstein shock absorbers, and oil cooler were all included in the 1976 East Coast base price of $25,880. The option list was short: electric sliding sunroof ($675), limited-slip differential ($345),

The Turbo Carrera—designated Type 930—debuted in Europe in 1975, with a 3.0-liter six-cylinder engine developing 234 bhp. It was packed with luxury features such as air conditioning, automatic heat control, stereo, and more.

heavy-duty starter ($50), and "Turbo" graphics ($120). The buyer could also specify custom paint for an additional $250. The Turbo came only as a coupe, and was never offered with Sportomatic, although several experimental cars were so equipped, and they worked well.

The turbocharger was placed on a cast-aluminum manifold studded to the heads, with Ultramid plastic tubes for the K-Jetronic fuel injection placed between manifold and inlet ports. Boost pressure was 0.8 atmospheres or 11.5 psi. The engine was a 2993cc version of the 911 flat six, the extra displacement chosen to produce the best possible off-boost torque

with the lower compression necessitated by the addition of the turbo. Though this power unit was admittedly less torquey below 3000 rpm than the 911S engine, things started to happen quickly after that. Published performance figures showed 0-60 mph times from 4.9 to 6.7 seconds and 0-100 mph times from 12.9 to 15.3 seconds, with standing-start quarter times between 13.5 and 15.2 seconds.

The 930's handling was basically that of a routine 911, but the Turbo was more stable at higher speeds, probably because of its larger rear tires and wider track. The Turbo had stiffer shocks and springs in addition to its wider rear wheels, so it didn't ride as

Type 930s had standard features such as electric antenna and window lifts, leather upholstery, tinted glass, headlamp washers, rear window wiper, Bilstein shocks, and oil cooler. Sunroof extra. Base price in 1976 was $25,880.

well as lesser Porsches. Steering was heavier, and tire noise from its Pirelli Cinturatos was considerable. Few complained about its brakes, which exhibited no fade, were impossible to lock, and were capable of bringing the car to a halt from 60 mph in under 160 feet. Above all, the 930 was a remarkably civilized car, particularly in view of its performance potential. The Turbo remained on the U.S. market through the 1979 model year, by which time its base price had risen to over $45,000.

TYPE 934

Racing developments also proceeded apace, and in 1975 another turbo—the Type 934—was introduced for FIA's Group 4 GT category. Its body was basically stock 911, but the fender flares were fiberglass, pop-riveted to the existing sheet metal, and the car had a huge front air dam as well as the "whale tail" spoiler out back. Some vestiges of the street car remained. In order to meet minimum Group 4 weight requirements, Porsche left in the power window lifts, door map compartments, and other luxury features. Turbo boost could be altered right from the cockpit via a control knob on the dash. In addition to the basic suspension, coil springs were mounted atop gas-filled Bilstein shock absorbers. Hard plastic bushings replaced rubber in the control arms. Adjustable anti-roll bars were provided front and rear, and Goodyear racing tires were fitted. The brakes came from none other than the 917, with drilled discs, finned wheel cylinders, and twin master cylinders. In order to meet the Group 4 requirements for a near-stock engine, the only changes from 930 specifications were in turbo boost pressure and camshaft timing and duration. One item of interest was a water cooling system—not for the engine, of course, but for the turbo-boosted air on its way to the cylinder head. This was necessary to prevent loss in volumetric efficiency. A water/alcohol mixture was used, and the cooler was mounted in the front air dam. Porsche built 31 of the 934 Turbo RSRs, and sold every one of them for $40,000 apiece.

TYPE 935

Then came the Type 935, yet a further development that barely resembled the 930, and compared to it in performance as a 911 does to a VW Beetle.

The car was designed for the Group 5 World Championship. Both the 934 and 935 took their last numbers of their designations from their GT racing classes. The 930 base was again used, because a ground-up racing car would not qualify: FIA had adopted new "silhouette" regulations, requiring cars to look "approximately" like the street versions—but only approximately. Two Type 935s were initially built. Hardly anything on them resembled the 930: doors, fenders, deck, hood, and spoilers were of fiberglass, and windows were of Plexiglass. So much weight was shaved, in fact, that Porsche had to add 150 pounds to bring the car back up to minimum—weight that Porsche would naturally want to add to the front of the car. Because the FIA allowed modified fenders, those of later 935s were utterly different from stock: aerodynamically low and smooth, with headlamps mounted in the huge air dam. Inside was a single deep bucket seat

Opposite page: An example of the Carrera RSR 3.0. Below: Aerodynamic nose, tail, and other aids gave the 935/78 a look that was quite a bit different from production turbos.

surrounded by the regulation roll cage. A large 8000-rpm tachometer dominated the instrument panel, flanked by boost pressure and other minor gauges. A central lever allowed the driver to adjust rear anti-roll bar stiffness as fuel diminished and weight distribution changed. The front anti-roll bar was also adjustable. The suspension comprised adjustable titanium coil springs up front (instead of the conventional torsion bars) and trailing arms at the rear. The brakes were basically conventional, but with extra cooling ducts, while the tires were an eye-popping 19 inches wide on 14½-inch rims. Front tire width was 16 inches.

Because the engine was turbocharged, the 935's displacement would be multiplied by a factor of 1.4 as a handicap. To keep it under the class limit of 4000cc, the engine was debored to 92mm, giving it an actual displacement of 2875cc. Bosch mechanical fuel injection replaced the K-Jetronic system of the production 930 Turbo. Also fitted were dual ignition and lightweight engine components, such as titanium conrods. Boost pressure was higher than stock—19 to 22 psi. The result was 590 bhp (DIN) at 7900 rpm, with 434 pounds-feet of torque peaking at 5400 rpm.

The 934 and 935 steps up from the 930 proved to have unbelievable performance figures. They reached 60 mph from standing still in under six seconds and under 3½ seconds, respectively. Climbing to 100 mph took a little over 10 seconds and a little over six, with the quarter-mile taking a tick over 14 seconds for the 934 and just under nine seconds for the 935.

Porsche was disappointed when IMSA initially banned turbocharged cars in 1976, for it destroyed possibilities for a championship in the Camel GT series. The ban was lifted at mid-year. Meanwhile, the cars did race in Trans-Am events, and won the

Today's Turbos have 3299cc flat sixes that develop 282 bhp. Interiors, following tradition, stress information and support.

championship that year for George Follmer (934), followed by Hurley Haywood, both from the Holbert Racing team. The 935 had similar bad luck with race organizers in Europe. After 935s had won the first two races of the European GT championship, the authorities demanded that the 930's spoiler must be fitted—requiring Porsche to adapt the 934's "waterworks" to provide proper cooling. Despite some faltering in mid-season, following the waterworks modifications and subsequent difficulties, Porsche pulled out the World Championship for Makes late in the season, outlasting the BMWs at Watkins Glen, New York. The first time the title had been won by a supercharged racing car, it signified a revolution in Group 5 racing: from then on, it took a turbocharger to win.

In subsequent years, Group 5 saw the advent of supercars from many manufacturers. In the mid-Eighties, Porsche would release another Group 5 entry that would again prove the standard—still based on the 911 silhouette.

Porsche built a great many more Turbos than it expected. From the initial homologation minimum of 500, production was up to around 1300 by the end of 1976. Today, the 911 Turbo carries on the tradition established by the earlier turbo-charged Porsches. Its 3299cc flat six develops

282 bhp (SAE), pushing a 2976-pound automobile. The factory claims 0-60 mph times in the mid-five-second range, with a claimed top speed of 157 mph. All of this and 22 mpg highway. Power, comfort, and a great racing heritage give the turbos—the 930, 934, 935, and today's 911 Turbo—more than enough standing among the all-time great automobiles.

MAJOR SPECIFICATIONS

1974 Porsche Carrera, 1976 Type 930, 1976 Type 934, 1976 Type 935, 1986 911 Turbo

General: Rear-engine, rear-drive, two-door sports coupe. Unit body production, steel frame competition

Dimensions and Capacities	1974 Carrera	1976 930	1976 934	1976 935	1986 911 Turbo
Wheelbase (in.):	89.3	89.3	89.3	89.3	89.5
Overall length (in.):	168.9	168.9	165.2	183.1	168.9
Overall width (in.):	63.4	69.9	73.6	78.6	69.9
Overall height (in.):	52.0	52.0	50.0	50.0	51.6
Track front (in.):	52.6	56.4	59.1	59.1	56.4
Track rear (in.):	51.8	59.1	60.4	61.4	58.7
Weight (lbs.):	2550 (curb)	2800 (curb)	2470 (dry)	2139 (dry)	2976 (curb)

Drivetrain

Engine type: Horizontally opposed 6-cylinder, air-cooled

	1974 Carrera	1976 930	1976 934	1976 935	1986 911 Turbo
Displacement (cc/ci):	2687/164	2993/183	2994/183	2856/174	3299/201
Compression ratio:	9.0:1	6.5:1	6.5:1	6.5:1	7.0:1
Fuel delivery:	Bosch CIS elect. fuel injection	Bosch CIS elect. fuel injection, turbo	Bosch K-Jetronic, turbo	Bosch plunger pump, turbo	Bosch CIS elect. fuel injection
Net bhp @ rpm:	175 @ 5800 DIN	245 @ 5500 DIN	485 @ 7000 DIN	590 @ 7900 DIN	282 @ 5500 SAE
Net lbs/ft torque@rpm:	na	246 @ 4500 SAE	na	na	278 @ 4000 SAE
Transmission type:	5-speed manual	4-speed manual	4-speed manual	4-speed manual	4-speed manual
Final drive ratio:	4.43:1	4.22:1	na	na	4.22:1

Chassis

Front suspension: MacPherson strut, lower A-arms, coil springs, transverse torsion bars, anti-roll bar; modifications for 934 and 935
Rear suspension: Semi-trailing arm, transverse torsion bars, anti-roll bar; modifications for 934 and 935
Steering: Rack-and-pinion
Brake system: 4-wheel disc brakes

	1974 Carrera	1976 930	1976 934	1976 935	1986 911 Turbo
Wheels:	15″	15″	16″	16″ front, 19″ rear	7J × 15″ front, 9J × 16″ rear
Tires:	185/70VR-15	185/70VR-15 front, 215/60VR-15 rear	Racing	Racing	205/55VR-16 front, 245/45VR-16 rear

Performance

	1974 Carrera	1976 930	1976 934	1976 935	1986 911 Turbo
0-60 mph (sec.):	na	na	na	na	5.5 (factory)
Top speed (mph):	na	na	na	200 (observed)	157 (factory)
EPA city mpg:	—	—	—	—	16
EPA highway mpg:	—	—	—	—	22

THE ULTIMATE 911: TYPE 959

The Porsche 959 resembles the 911 in silhouette, but the body's proportions are different.

THE BASIS

Taking its Group 5 competition efforts an evolutionary step further, Porsche began running an all-new unit in the mid-Eighties. The Type 959 was developed to compete in rallying, and its record has shown that the goals for the capabilities of the car have been met. In order for it to qualify for Group B, 200 roadworthy units of the 959 had to be offered by Porsche. The fortunate few to own one got sophisticated electronics, hydraulics, and bodywork for the approximate $195,000 that they had to pay—a far cry from the near-$5000 base-model price of the first 911/912s in the mid-Sixties.

Perhaps the best description of the 959's appearance is that it obviously was derived from the 911's styling. Window glass and the roofline were the strongest direct visual carry-overs from the established model, but other than that, Porsche's engineering was about all that was held in common by the two types. Development was virtually from scratch. While the body looked like it was a 911 body, the proportions were different. Porsche could have shaped it in any manner desired, but apparently wanted the identification afforded by the 911-like shape. The central thrust of the aerodynamics applied to the body shape was to reduce lift as much as possible, with a low drag coefficient of importance, also. Using 1/5-scale models and then full-scale ones in wind tunnels, a body was shaped that combined aesthetic beauty with lift-free, low-drag aerodynamics (0.32 Cd). The body was also built for strength and for light weight, employing such

high-tech materials as aluminum alloys, polyurethane, and aramid-fiber compound for the skin and galvanized steel for the rigid safety-cell framework. The body was flexible where necessary, such as in the area of the polyurethane front spoiler, and rust resistant in others, such as in the frame. Along the bottom of the car, a flat pan reduced air turbulence and contributed to the lack of lift on the body. All in all, the 959 looked to all the world like an Eighties and Nineties 911, with gorgeous curves, spoilers, and air dams that could carry the 911 style into the years (perhaps decades) ahead.

THE DRIVETRAIN

In the engineering of the 959's turbocharged powerplant, certain goals were foremost in the minds of the development team: The engine should be capable of good acceleration and high power output at the top end of the rpm range, as well as being as fuel-efficient as possible. Usually, turbocharging an engine gives it added muscle, but low-rpm power and its initial acceleration capabilities are relatively flat. The problem is in waiting for the turbo to kick in so that it can be effective. Small turbo-

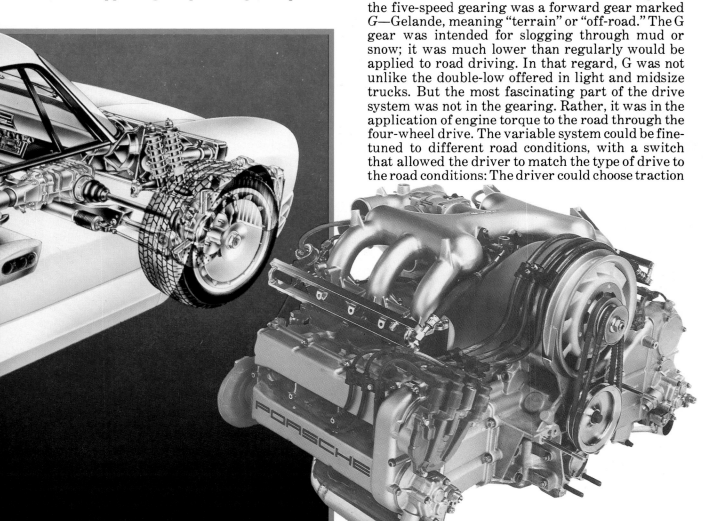

chargers alleviate some of the problems caused by waiting to overcome the inertia of a larger one, but the responsiveness comes at the expense of not being able to achieve maximum torque and nonefficient use of fuel. Porsche engineered a more balanced system that had two turbochargers that worked in two stages. One of the turbos was set up to receive a constant flow of exhaust gas in a more or less "normal" application of the technology, despite the Rube Goldberg type of plumbing. That plumbing initially sent all of the exhaust gases to only the one turbo. Then, in the upper engine-speed range, the plumbing was electronically controlled to allow the second turbocharger to kick in and to share equally in the production of boosted air for the engine. Aiding in the efficiency of the turbocharging system, two large air-to-air intercoolers were part of the plumbing—they were situated at the engine's flanks. The 2850cc horizontally opposed six-cylinder engine developed 450 brake horsepower at 6500 rpm.

The rest of the drivetrain was just as complex. The engine coupled to the transaxle via a six-speed gearbox. Half-shafts turned the rear wheels, and the transaxle continued to the front wheels. Along with the five-speed gearing was a forward gear marked *G*—Gelande, meaning "terrain" or "off-road." The G gear was intended for slogging through mud or snow; it was much lower than regularly would be applied to road driving. In that regard, G was not unlike the double-low offered in light and midsize trucks. But the most fascinating part of the drive system was not in the gearing. Rather, it was in the application of engine torque to the road through the four-wheel drive. The variable system could be fine-tuned to different road conditions, with a switch that allowed the driver to match the type of drive to the road conditions: The driver could choose traction

(locked), ice and snow, wet, and dry settings. In addition, wheel sensors detected slip, and through a hydraulic system, electronics increased the contact force of the wheels where it was most needed. Evaluations took place in a continuing process. The variable four-wheel drive could distribute the torque from anywhere between a 50-percent split front and rear to all of it applied at the rear wheels.

In addition to the microprocessed torque-splitting, another system raised and lowered the suspension of the car. The leveling was in response to the different conditions encountered in rallying, including everything from off-road conditions (for which the top setting cleared the ground by almost

Opposite page, top: Full rally version of the 959—the 961—has been a success. Below and bottom: The 959's lines give it a 0.32 Cd. Various scoops cool brakes, engine, intercoolers. Production version features wide range of suspension and drive configuration adjustments.

2½ inches above its normal setting) to high-speed paved surfaces. Should the driver have neglected to reduce the height when passing from rougher terrain to smoother, increasing speed correspondingly, the micros made sure that the body lowered closer to the road proportionally. Another automatically adjusted part of the car was its shock absorber system: Shock rate, too, could be varied, from soft to firm, in accordance with the type of driving that was being done. The ride became firmer as the speed increased, if necessary changes in the settings were ignored by the driver.

The tires and wheels were special, also. Behind the flush wheel covers, the magnesium wheels had

spokes that were hollow, opening into the wheel rim and, consequently, the tires. Two pressure switches were built into the rims to monitor air pressure, maintaining an electronic watch system that reported loss of air pressure on a dashboard gauge. The gauge indicated exactly which tire was losing pressure. At the same time, the 235/40VR-17 front and 255/40VR-17 rear Dunlop Denloc tires mounted on the hollow-spoked wheels were designed to maintain their hold on the rims in case of a blowout, helping the driver to control the car at high speeds. The

wheels and tires complemented the anti-lock braking system used on the car.

The various systems operating as parts of the chassis and drivetrain planted the 959 into something like Tomorrow Land. Crossing from rough dirt road to high-speed autobahn brought into play the full range of the automatic leveling, shock settings, variable four-wheel drive, and, without doubt, shifting of stages in turbocharging from the double-turbocharged engine. The car seemed to be as computerized as a spacecraft!

THE INTERIOR

Interior appointments reflected their heritage, having been popped from the same mold as the 911 seats, dash, and general layout. Yet, for its familiarity, the interior was entirely new. The tachometer took up the center part of the instrument cluster, flanked by gauges and lights on the right and left. Unique to the 959, though, were the lights for the low-air-pressure sensors, the controls for the variable drive setting, and those for the shocks and leveling on the console. The super Porsche was conceived as a long-distance traveler, as its electronically controlled environment attested. Leather trim matched the color of the exterior.

Top: At its road-racing debut in the 1986 Le Mans 24-Hour, a 961 driven by Rene Metge and Claude Ballot-Lena finished seventh. Bottom: Air-cooled engine, water-cooled cylinder heads, and two air-to-air intercoolers.

THE ULTIMATE 911

The competition versions of the 959—the 961s—have proven themselves in some of the roughest World Championship rallying events. Tractable in city driving, the 959s could be the world's fastest production cars, with top speed estimated to be over 200 mph. But that's fodder for another cannon.

Significant changes have been applied to the Porsche line since the introduction of the 356s. While the 911s have continued to ensure Porsche's niche in automotive history, the 959s go beyond to thrust the company's reputation into the future.

MAJOR SPECIFICATIONS

Porsche Type 959	
General: Rear-engine, variable four-wheel-drive, two-door coupe. **Base price:** Est. $195,000	
Dimensions and Capacities	
Wheelbase (in.):	90.3
Overall length (in.):	167.7
Curb weight (lbs.):	Est. 2975
Fuel tank (gal.):	23.8
Drivetrain	
Engine type: Horizontally opposed dohc 6-cylinder, 4 valves per cylinder, air cooled, water-cooled cylinder heads	
Displacement (cc/ci):	2850/174
Compression ratio:	8.0:1
Fuel delivery: Individual cylinder injection, two injectors per cylinder. twin 2-stage turbocharging with 2 air-to-air intercoolers	
Net bhp @ rpm:	450 @ 6500
Transmission type:	6-speed manual
Final drive ratio:	4.12:1
Chassis	
Front and rear suspension: Dual transverse arms and dual shock absorbers, adjustable shock stiffness and ride level	
Brake system: Anti-lock brake system, 4-piston brake calipers on ventilated disc brakes	
Wheels: Hollow-spoke magnesium, with center-lock hubs **Tires:** Denloc, 235/40VR-17 front, 255/40VR-17 rear	
Performance	
0-60 mph (sec.):	Est. 4.0
Top speed (mph):	Est. 180 +

911 CONVERSIONS

CUSTOM 911s

A s if the factory Porsche 911s and their variants weren't enough, coachbuilders have been at work over the years custom-tailoring the sports cars to their customers' tastes and budgets. Attempting to reach a little higher speed, to add to the 911's basic shape, or to affect the suspension and handling or level of luxury in the interior, the masters of conversions have done everything from making racing 935s street legal to adding enough leather, plastic, and fiberglass to almost disguise the car.

Some of the attempts have proven successful, and the conversions are among the more desired automobiles in the world today. Here are some of the best of these unique machines.

A.I.R.

Founded in 1970, American International Racing of Burbank, California, specializes in fiberglass conversion parts and suspension components for the street and the race track. A.I.R. designs and manufactures its own fiberglass and suspension parts. Slant noses, grilles, air dams, whale tails, bumpers, valances, rear quarter panels with side vents, wheels, and stripes can all be found in the A.I.R. catalog, along with instrumentation and lighting accessories. Total racing kits for 935, GTO, and GTU conversions are among the company's offerings, as well as RS, RSR, and IROC parts. Steel conversion kits are also available from A.I.R.

D.E.C.I. MOTORSPORTS

Located in Buena Park, California, D.E.C.I. has full customizing facilities, with the capabilities of doing everything from shipping aftermarket and original-equipment parts and accessories to tackling the full conversion of a customer's car. Complete modifications of 911s to have steel slant noses or to turn them into cabriolets are possible, or the parts for such conversions can be shipped directly to a customer so that he can do his own work. D.E.C.I. prides itself in the gold-plated articles that it produces. Alarms, wood dashes, floor mats, wheels, and leather accessories can be ordered.

DP MOTORSPORT

West German Ekkehard Zimmerman, dp motor-sport's founder, began by building homemade cars based on Volkswagen Beetle chassis. However, his first choice was to work with Porsches. So after a stint with Ford Motor Company of Germany as a designer, he started Design + Plastic, later abbreviated to dp, designing conversion kits for 911s and

then RSR street Porsches. Zimmerman's crafts-manship brought him to the attention of Porsche-Shop Kremer. Together, they put together very successful endurance GT prototype cars, winning the Le Mans 24-Hour in 1979. Eventually, German sports car racing allowed more creative bodywork on "production" cars, and dp built Porsches with large front air dams and integrated headlights. The current conversions offered by Ekkehard Zimmer-

man's dp motorsport evolved from the company's background in racing and building track-inspired road versions of 911-based Porsches. Dp 935 I and dp 935 II are currently available, with the turbo-charged cabriolet having up to 380 horsepower. The cabrio is structurally reinforced. Brakes and wheels have been modified. Turbo boost level is controlled by the driver.

GEMBALLA INTERNATIONAL

The epitome of Gemballa's Porsche conversions is the Avalanche, which can run well over $200,000 if the right options are ordered. Another company based in West Germany (near Stuttgart), Gemballa modifies the exteriors and the interiors of the 911s placed in its hands. The Avalanche has a tail section full of functional arabesques, extra-width flares, aerodynamic mirror housings, slant-nose front, a wild baked-enamel finish, and heat-reflective windows. Inside, leather can be found everywhere, covering seats, dashboard, door panels, and trimming the carpets. Matching leather luggage is in the trunk. Electrically operated seats, computerized instrumentation, a heavy-duty air conditioning system, and a remote-control stereo system give the driver an extremely comfortable environment. The 500-watt stereo system includes radio, cassette, and

compact disc player—all controlled from the steering wheel hub. The Ruf-turbocharged engine can take the Avalanche to over 180 miles per hour. If the Avalanche is a little too much for your budget, lower-priced series of Gemballa conversions start between $75,000 and $115,000.

KREMER

Kremer is noted for its outstanding work in prototype endurance and other racing endeavors. A 935 Kremer shows how the German company's racing cars translate to street use. Four headlights in an air dam, a biplane rear wing, running boards with air slots, rear slotted fenders, and a sunroof are some of the Kremer car's exterior touches. Inside, power windows and air conditioning are part of an environment that also holds an electronically variable turbo boost control. Using full boost takes the engine up to 478 brake horsepower. Handling the car's contact with the road are tires with widths of 225 front and 285 rear and with rims measuring 11 inches front and 13 inches rear. The 935 Kremer rides on a racing suspension.

RINSPEED DESIGN

Rinspeed—founded in 1976 by Frank M. Rinder-knecht—began by converting various cars. Porsches began receiving the greatest share of the company's attention in 1982. The three models based on the 911 are designated 939, 969, and 979. The 939 is a Carrera cabriolet body powered by a 911 Turbo engine. The 969 takes the 911 Turbo a little further than the factory did. The slanted nose has a small wing across it, and extended air ducts along the sides feed air to the rear brakes and engine. Turbocharger boost may be increased for added horsepower. Both the 939 and 969 are sold only as complete automobiles. The 979 conversion pieces can be purchased in kit form.

RUF AUTOMOBILES

The manufacturing company now bearing the Ruf name began as a mechanical repair shop in 1939 by Louis Ruf's father. As a result of the younger Ruf's interest in the 911, the company builds five-speed transmissions, engine modification kits, turbochargers, intercoolers, suspension upgrades, and 17-inch tires, and it offers other accessories. However, the most important offerings from Ruf are its 25 complete cars per year—turbo coupes at about $115,000 and turbo cabriolets $10,000 to $15,000 above that. While Porsche doesn't make a turbo cabriolet, Ruf does—with a five-speed manual (something else that Porsche doesn't offer with a turbo engine). Top speed: over 185.

THE 911 AFTERMARKET

A small sampling of the countless items relating to the Porsche 911 that are available in the marketplace— parts, accessories, and memorabilia.

Cabrio Turbo-Look

Parts and accessories available from Porsche include those that give a cabriolet the look of a 911 Turbo. Dr. Ing.h.c.F. Porsche Aktiengesellschaft, Postfach 40 06 40, 7000 Stuttgart 40, West Germany; (0711) 827-0.

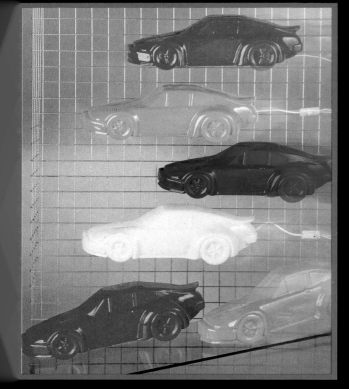

Porsche Lamp

Gleaming with the speed of light. Available in red, yellow, blue, and white. Size is 20 inches by six inches. $60.00. L'art et L'automobile, 354 East 66th Street, New York, New York 10021; 212/772-1665.

Porsche Softies
Comfortable pillows detailed to the rotating wheels. 16 inches long by eight inches wide by six inches tall. Red or yellow. $39.00, plus $2.50 shipping. Ambient Shapes, Inc., P.O. Box 5069, Hickory, North Carolina 28603; 800/438-2244.

Slope Nose 930
Model in approximately 1/24 scale is made of wood, having turned aluminum wheels with centers of etched brass. Fender flares of styrene. Limited edition of five. $750.00. Co-Hog Toys, 62 Reservoir Street, Norton, Massachusetts 02766; 617/285-6337.

Sterling Silver Key Chain
German handmade. Two inches long. $199.95. Also gold or platinum. Beverly Hills Motoring Accessories, 200 South Robertson Boulevard, Beverly Hills, California 90211; 800/421-0911, 213/657-4800.

EINMALIG!

PORSCHE 930 CABRIOLET

WILLHOIT GRAPHICS POSTERS·CALIFORNIA 90804·USA·©1983

Porsche Posters
Complete line of Porsche-related
posters, each mailed in tube.
P.B. Tweeks, Ltd., 4410 North
Keystone Avenue, Indianapolis,
Indiana 46205; 800/428-2200
(Indianapolis), 800/241-6227
(Norcross, Georgia),
800/421-3776 (Signal Hill,
California).

Bauer Classic Car Kits
Porsche 911SC kits are made of solid white pine and
have a clear finish, emphasizing the various grains
and colors of the wood. The Porsche kits are easy to
build. They weigh about eight pounds and are 18⅞
inches long. $169.98 suggested retail price.
International Hobbies Corporation, 350 East
Tioga Street, Philadelphia, Pennsylvania 19134;
215/426-2873.

Saratoga Tops in Lexan
Shaded tops of General Electric super-tough Lexan for 911 Targa require no drilling, adaptors, or body modifications. Complete with fittings and weatherstrips. P.B. Tweeks, Ltd., 4410 North Keystone Avenue, Indianapolis, Indiana 46205; 800/428-2200 (Indianapolis), 800/241-6227 (Norcross, Georgia), 800/421-3776 (Signal Hill, California).

Auto Vest
A wide variety of custom designed vests for Porsches and other import and American automobiles are made of high-quality materials with soft scratch-resistant backing. George Stevens Manufacturing Co., 20390 Carlton Creek Road, Florence, Montana 59833; 800/523-9834.

t Junior
ube chassis with reinforced
asuring 85 inches long with
e. Two-stroke 50cc engine
epower. Maximum speed
Autojunios S. Zaccaria,
4/554227, Telex 551297

Whale tails, rocker panel kits
rear valances available. Di
of fiberglass and steel. P. B.
North Keystone Avenue, Ind
46205; 800/428-2
800/241-6227 (N
800/421-3776 (Sign